U.S. ACRES

RUNS AMUCK

TOPPER BOOKS

AN IMPRINT OF PHAROS BOOKS • A SCRIPPS HOWARD COMPANY

NEW YORK

Library of Congress Catalog Card Number: 88-064012
Pharos ISBN: 0-88687-437-8

Printed in United States of America

Topper Books
An Imprint of Pharos books
A Scripps Howard Company
200 Park Avenue
New York, NY 10166

10 9 8 7 6 5 4 3 2

WADE'S WORST FEARS

1. WATER IN ANY FORM, INCLUDING ICE, WATERMELONS, AND JACQUES COUSTEAU SPECIALS

2. SLEEPING WITH HIS EYES CLOSED

3. DUCK-EATING RECLINERS

4. BEING TRAMPLED IN A HAMSTER STAMPEDE

5. SITTING ON A LIZARD

TIME TO DECORATE THE CHRISTMAS TREE

WHOOPS! THAT'S A LITTLE LOPSIDED...

UH-OH...TOO MUCH THE OTHER WAY!

PERFEEECT!

AND NOW FOR THE FINISHING TOUCH

JIM DAVIS 12-20

OOOOOOOOO OOOOOOOO

JIM DAVIS 1-17

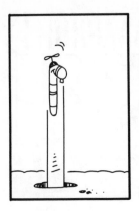

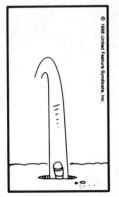

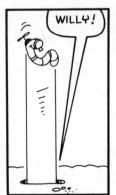

WILLY!

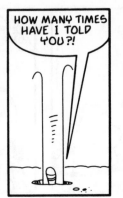

HOW MANY TIMES HAVE I TOLD YOU?!

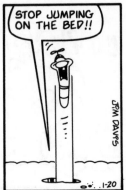

STOP JUMPING ON THE BED!!

JIM DAVIS

1-20

HEY, CODY, YOU'RE A HUNTING DOG AREN'T YOU?

YEAH!

YOU WANT TO HUNT SOME **WORMS** WITH ME?!

ALL RIGHT!

UH-OH

JIM DAVIS 1-21

LET'S GO!

HEY, BOOKER?

WHAT **ARE** WORMS?

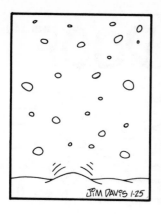

© 1988 United Feature Syndicate, Inc.

JIM DAVIS 2-1

HI, BANANA BEAK!

HI, BANANA BEAK!

WHAT **IS** ALL THIS "BANANA-BEAK" STU-

© 1988 United Feature Syndicate, Inc.

HAR-HAR-HAR!

JIM DAVIS 2-2

CHOMP!

WHOA THERE, PARDNER!

JIM DAVIS 2-10

OH, HONEY, I'M HOME!

WHY DIDN'T YOU WIPE YOUR FEET?! NOW YOU'VE TRACKED DIRT INTO THE HOUSE!!

WHAT ARE YOU TALKING ABOUT?! WE LIVE IN DIRT!

AND, I DON'T EVEN HAVE FEET!

YOU DON'T HAVE TO SHOUT

JIM DAVIS 2-11

PANT
PANT
PANT

© 1988 United Feature Syndicate, Inc.

JIM DAVIS 2-12

PARDON ME, YOUNG MAN. DID YOU SEE MY POODLE, FIFI, COME BY HERE?

YOU KNOW, WHEN MY TIME COMES, I WANNA GO IN STYLE!

© 1988 United Feature Syndicate, Inc.

LIKE MY UNCLE ED!

HOW DID HE GO?

HE WENT FISHING

JIM DAVIS 2-13

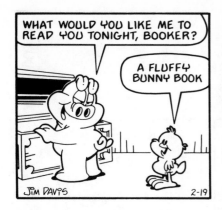

DOOF

BOOF THONK

JIM DAVIS

2-24

HEY, SHELDON, ARE YOU GONNA COME WATCH ME PRACTICE MY SKIING TODAY?

I GUESS I'D BETTER

WELL, HURRY UP!

JUST A SECOND

JIM DAVIS

2-25

HA-HA, VERY FUNNY!

WOYOYOYOYNG!

ZIP

SCREEEE

ORSON! I GOT IT FIGURED OUT! IF I GO FAST ENOUGH, I CAN RACE RIGHT BY DANGER BEFORE IT CAN DO ANYTHING TO ME!

WELL, GOTTA RUSH!

© 1988 United Feature Syndicate, Inc.

WHAP

JIM DAVIS 3-2

HI, BIRD

NNGGGGHHH

YOU KNOW SOMETIMES YOU CAN BE REALLY IRRITATING

© 1988 United Feature Syndicate, Inc.

SMACK
SMACK
SLAP
SLAP
SLAP
SMACK
SMACK
SLAP

TAKE NOW, FOR INSTANCE

JIM DAVIS 3-3

GEE...

I WONDER WHAT I'LL LOOK LIKE WHEN I GROW UP

© 1988 United Feature Syndicate, Inc.

JIM DAVIS 3-11

CLICK CLICK CLICK

AH-HAA!

CLICKETY CLICK CLICKETY CLICKETY CLICK CLICKETY CLICK CLICK CLICK CLICK

© 1988 United Feature Syndicate, Inc.

JIM DAVIS 3-12

3-13

FFFFFF

BLAT!

CARE TO JOIN ME IN MEDITATION, LANOLIN?

SURE

SHAPE UP, UNIVERSE!

THAT'S ENOUGH ENLIGHTENMENT FOR ONE DAY. YOU CAN TAKE IT FROM HERE, EGG

PEACE BE WITH YOU

FLUFF FLUFF FLUFF

© 1988 United Feature Syndicate, Inc.

BEDTIME, CODY
OKAY, BLUE

Z

JIM DAVIS 3-28

HEY, ORSON, LOOK AT CODY TWITCHING IN HIS SLEEP
HE'S DREAMING
Z

© 1988 United Feature Syndicate, Inc.

WHAT DO YOU SUPPOSE HE'S DREAMING ABOUT?

SNAP

HUNTING, I'D SAY

JIM DAVIS 3-29

© 1988 United Feature Syndicate, Inc.

© 1988 United Feature Syndicate, Inc.

BOOF!

WHIZZZZ

GRAB

© 1988 United Feature Syndicate, Inc.

WHIZZZZZ

JIM DAVIS 4-8

AH-CHOO!

© 1988 United Feature Syndicate, Inc.

-CHOO
CHOO
CHOO
CHOO
CHOO
CHOO
CHOO
CHOO

IT'S BAD ENOUGH SNEEZING IN HERE, BUT THE ECHO IS MURDER!

JIM DAVIS 4-9

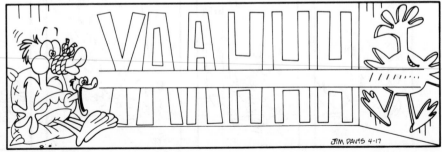

ZIP

THOONK

GRAB

YANK

© 1988 United Feature Syndicate, Inc.

WHAT THE—

DON'T ASK

JIM DAVIS 4-24

© 1988 United Feature Syndicate, Inc.

JIM DAVIS 5-18

© 1988 United Feature Syndicate, Inc.

ZIP

SLAM

JIM DAVIS 5-19

SNAP

© 1988 United Feature Syndicate, Inc.

JIM DAVIS 5-20

HOT ENOUGH FOR YOU TODAY, BO?

WHY, HOW KIND OF YOU TO ASK AND TO BE CONCERNED, ORSON! YES, IT IS QUITE WARM ENOUGH FOR ME TODAY, THANK YOU. BUT, ENOUGH ABOUT ME. WHAT ABOUT YOU?

© 1988 United Feature Syndicate, Inc.

IS IT HOT ENOUGH FOR YOU TODAY, ORSON?

YUP

JIM DAVIS 5-21

5-30

JIM DAVIS

© 1988 United Feature Syndicate, Inc.

5-31

JIM DAVIS

YEEEEK!

WHONK

LANOLIN, BE HONEST, WHAT DO YOU THINK OF ME?

YOU ARE AN OBNOXIOUS, EGOCENTRIC, COLDHEARTED, LOUDMOUTHED BULLY

YOU DON'T HAVE TO SUGAR-COAT IT. LIST SOME OF MY FAULTS, TOO

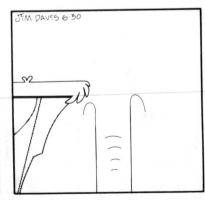

© 1988 United Feature Syndicate, Inc.

JFM DAVIS 7-10

© 1988 United Feature Syndicate, Inc.

JIM DAVIS 7-11

UH-OH, HERE COMES THAT CHICKEN! I'D BETTER GO INTO MY FLAWLESS CHOPSTICK IMPRESSION

HI, MR. CHICKEN

HI, MISTER CHOPSTICK

© 1988 United Feature Syndicate, Inc.

MISTER CHOPSTICK?!!

JIM DAVIS 7-12

1988 United Feature Syndicate. Inc

JIM DAVIS 7-13

I CAN'T BELIEVE SOME OF THE THINGS FOR SALE IN THIS FARM CATALOGUE!

LIKE WHAT?

LIKE ELECTRIC CATTLE PRODS!

WOW!

© 1988 United Feature Syndicate. Inc

ELECTRIC CATTLE! WHAT'LL THEY THINK OF NEXT?

JIM DAVIS 7-14

WHAT DID THE CHICKEN SAY WHEN SHE LAID THE SQUARE EGG?

I DON'T KNOW, WHAT?

© 1988 United Feature Syndicate, Inc.

YEEEEOOOOWCH!!

JIM DAVIS 7-15

ZIP

YEEEK!

© 1988 United Feature Syndicate, Inc.

A MOUSE!

JIM DAVIS 7-16